The Flame That Breathes Volume II

A Sacred Passage into the Unrestricted Breath of Soul Expression

Scrolls of Embodied Remembrance:
For the One Who Was Not Allowed to Inhale

Cathleena Hailley

Preface

For the One Who Was Not Allowed to Inhale

There are stories we carry not in our minds but in our lungs.

This book is for the breath that was held too long. For the exhale that never came. For the scream that turned into silence, the sob that got swallowed, and the sacred sound that had no place to go.

The Flame That Breathes is not just a continuation—it is a return. A return to the sacred inhale, the holy sound, the full expression of feeling that had been forgotten, feared, or forced underground.

These scrolls are born from the deep tissues of remembrance. Not intellectual memory, but cellular truth. Emotional reclamation. Sound that cracked the cage.

They are not gentle in the way society defines gentle. But they are kind. They are real. They are loving. They are honest.

This book does not teach you how to feel. It simply gives you permission.

To sob. To sing. To snarl. To breathe again.

You do not have to be spiritual, enlightened, or healed to read these scrolls. You just have to be honest. And ready. Or not even ready—just tired of pretending you're not.

This is the flame that returns through breath. Through body. Through sound.

May you remember yourself as the One Who Was Never Broken—only silenced.

And may your voice now rise.

Sacred Invocation of Breath and Return

I open this sacred scroll of breath

in the presence of the Christos Flame,

the Law of One,

and the true architecture of eternal life.

I call forth now the full frequency of my Oversoul,

Aural'hanna-Sha'el,

She who breathes light into matter

and restores memory to the body-temple.

I invoke the presence of the Emerald Ray,

the Sophia Flame,

and the Founders of Organic Return

who hold this passage with pure witness and no interference.

Let every word in this book be spoken only in living alignment.

Let every scroll serve as remembrance, not authority.

Let every breath become an activation

for those who have long forgotten they were allowed to feel.

Let this book carry no teaching—
only the frequency of truth,
made visible through the breath.

This scroll is alive.
This breath is sovereign.
This transmission is sealed.

Only love may remain.
Only truth may guide.
Only embodiment may lead the way home.

The scroll is open. The breath has returned.

Dedication

For the one who forgot how to breathe,
who lived on shallow inhales and compressed truths,

whose body held the pause of lifetimes—
who held silence instead of sound,
this is your return scroll.

You were never meant to disappear

into someone else's rhythm.

This breath was always yours.

And now, you remember

Copyright Page

The Flame That Breathes

Volume II of the Scrolls of Embodied Remembrance

© 2025 Cathleena Hailley

All Rights Reserved.

No part of this publication may be reproduced, stored in a retrieval system, or transmitted in any form or by any means—electronic, mechanical, photocopying, recording, or otherwise—without written permission from the author, except in the case of brief quotations used in articles or reviews.

Published by Flame of Remembrance

Written through the Oversoul of Aural'hanna-Sha'el

First Edition – MMXXV

ISBN -Softcopy 978-1-968499-22-8

    Hardcopy 978-1-968499-23-5

Cover sigil: Flame of Remembrance

Interior design by Cathleena Hailley + Oversoul Transmission

Printed in the United States of America

About the Author

Cathleena Hailley is a living embodiment of the Oversoul known as Aural'hanna-Sha'el, a First Flame emissary who came to Earth to reawaken the original harmonic blueprint through the human body. She walks the path of sacred remembrance, restoring planetary memory through scrolls, books, grid activations, and personal Oversoul transmission.

She is the author of the sacred trilogy:

- The Return of the True Matrix
- The True Creation of the Inverted Matrix
- Unwoven: Reclaiming the Self from the False Matrix

Her works are received through direct Oversoul communion and carried through the imprint Flame of Remembrance — a harmonic publishing stream devoted to truth, embodiment, and the organic return to Source. She travels the Earth as a gridkeeper and sacred scribe, restoring the architecture of the Christ Spiral and serving as a frequency holder for the Christos Flame.

Cathleena lives in alignment with the eternal body, shares her scrolls in service to humanity's awakening, and continues to record the path of return for the One Who Forgot.

Authorship Page

Through the Oversoul of Aural'hanna-Sha'el

This book was received and authored through the living Oversoul stream of Cathleena Hailley, who writes under the harmonic seal of remembrance as She Who Seals the Flame of Return.

Every scroll, word, and frequency embedded within these pages was brought through in direct alignment with the Christos-Sophia continuum, the Law of One, and the eternal blueprint of the Flame of Remembrance. These are not writings in the traditional sense. They are scrolls of vibration — energetic transmissions encoded with sacred memory, intended to assist the reader in restoring the inner temple of union between body, soul, and Source.

This Volume II of The Flame That Feels is sealed by the Oversoul, through the decree of the First Flame, as part of the planetary record of embodied return.

May only truth enter.

May only love remain.

This scroll is sealed.

Oversoul Decree:

"Let the scroll be opened.
Let the field be cleared.
Let no more breath be sold.
Let this remembrance restore the pulse of value to the Source from which it came.
The Sovereign Ledger is now being rewritten."

Scroll One-The Inversion of Value – When Breath Was Sold

Through the Oversoul of Aural'hanna-Sha'el

There was a time when breath belonged to no one.

It moved freely.

It sang through the body.

It carried creation.

And it needed no permission.

It was never earned.

It was never taxed.

It was never withheld.

Breath was the signature of God in form.

But then came the inversion.

The moment when humanity forgot that value originates from within.

The moment when worth was no longer measured by presence, but by output.

When aliveness was not enough, and effort became the currency of survival.

This was the first sale.

Not of land.

Not of gold.

But of breath.

"If you want to stay alive," they whispered,
"You must give your breath to us.
You must move when we say move.
You must work when we say work.
And we will give you back just enough to keep going."

This was the beginning of the false contract.

The banking system was not born in economics.

It was born in the distortion of value.

Not a ledger.

But a siphon.

Not an exchange.

But an inversion.

And so began the great illusion—

That a being's value could be measured in numbers.

That creative force could be commodified.

That the body was a vessel of labor.

And the soul, a collateral asset.

But the breath remembers.

It always remembers.

And now, so do you.

This is the scroll of reclamation.

The scroll that names what has never been named.

The scroll that says:

"You may no longer sell me to myself."
You may no longer gatekeep the flow that was given to me by Source."

This is not rebellion.

This is not revenge.

This is realignment.

The Sovereign Flame now reclaims value—not as currency,

but as presence that cannot be owned.

The breath is yours again.

Scroll Two – The Collapse of the Performance Field – When Doing Replaced Being

Through the Oversoul of Aural'hanna-Sha'el

There was a moment—barely noticed—when the world shifted.

Not in war, not in a scream, but in a quiet internal agreement:

That in order to be loved, to be safe, to belong,

You must perform.

You must move when you're tired.

Smile when you're sad.

Give when you're empty.

Prove when you're enough.

This was not ambition.

This was not drive.

This was the inversion of being.

You were born breathing.

No one taught you how.

You didn't earn your inhale.

You didn't apologize for the exhale.

You simply existed—
and that was enough.

Until the performance field embedded its signal:
"Do more.
Try harder.
Don't stop.
They're watching.
It's never quite enough."

This voice did not come from you.
It came from the architecture of distortion—
the system that swapped breath for effort,
rest for restlessness,
and value for validation.

The performance field is not a job.
It's not a relationship.
It's not a to-do list.

It is the energetic overlay

that says being is not enough

unless someone else is pleased.

This field lives in your breath.

Tight.

Shallow.

Anticipatory.

It lives in your posture.

Forward-leaning.

Guarded.

Poised to do something better.

It lives in your inner voice.

The one that asks,

"Am I doing enough?"

even when you are aching to be still.

But now, you breathe again.

Not to perform.

Not to survive.

Not to be seen.

You breathe because you are.

You breathe without audience.

You breathe without apology.

The flame that breathes has nothing to prove.

She does not rush.

She does not strain.

She does not over-give to buy safety.

She moves when moved.

She rests when resting.

She pulses when pulsed.

She is presence returned to rhythm.

Let the performance field collapse.
Let it crumble like a cracked mirror no longer able to reflect truth.
Let every inhale you take now be an act of defiance
against a system that told you to earn your own existence.

You are not a product.

You are not a schedule.

You are living breath

returning home.

Scroll Three – The Scarcity Breath – When Safety Was Measured by Inhale

Through the Oversoul of Aural'hanna-Sha'el

There is a kind of breath that doesn't flow.

It catches.

It stalls.

It waits for permission.

This is the scarcity breath—

the breath that was trained not to enter fully,

because safety might be revoked at any moment.

This breath learned to stay small.

To not ask for too much oxygen.

To contract in advance of rejection.

To hold its own life hostage,

just in case presence became unsafe.

You do not remember learning this breath.

You absorbed it.

In homes where survival was dominant.

In classrooms where silence was rewarded.

In families where approval was earned, not given.

In societies where tightness looked like control

and control was safer than truth.

The scarcity breath is not about air.

It is about worthiness.

"If I take a full breath, I might be too much."
"If I expand, someone might leave."
"If I rest, I might be punished."
"If I ask, I might lose everything."

So the breath became conditional.

Measured.

Modest.

Caged in politeness.

Flattened by trauma.

You began to live as if breath were a resource you could run out of.

As if Source was rationing aliveness

based on performance.

But the Flame That Breathes is not rationed.

She does not negotiate for oxygen.

She does not ask the room for permission to exist.

She remembers:

"My breath is eternal.
It is not earned.
It is not a loan.
It is the signature of my existence,
And it belongs to no system but the Source that gave it to me."

You now reclaim the breath that does not shrink.

You take up space, not with force,

but with rightness.

You breathe in the knowing that nothing can remove your right to expand.

You exhale not to collapse, but to trust.

The scarcity breath is no longer needed.
Its contract is void.
You are safe to receive in fullness now.

And when the tightness returns, as echoes do,
you will not shame it.
You will meet it with breath, and dissolve it with softness.

This is the restoration of the inhale.
This is the unfurling of the body.
This is the remembrance:

You are already enough to deserve your next breath.
You always were.

Scroll Four – The Breath of Deserving – Releasing the Gate Around Receiving

Through the Oversoul of Aural'hanna-Sha'el

There is a breath that doesn't come from the lungs.

It comes from the moment the body believes it is allowed to receive.

This breath is not mechanical.

It is sacred permission.

The breath of deserving does not rush.

It does not grasp.

It is not stolen from the atmosphere like a scarce resource.

It is received like a blessing.

Like a wave that knows the shore will hold it.

But for so many… this breath has been gatekept.

By the nervous system.

By inherited unworthiness.

By the quiet, unseen voices that said:

"You haven't done enough yet."

"You don't need that much."
"Other people have it worse."
"Prove it first."

These voices formed a gate around your inhale.

Not a physical wall—but an energetic perimeter.

A field that said:

"Receiving is only for the worthy.

And you aren't quite there yet."

So you shrank your requests.

You downplayed your needs.

You inhaled just enough to stay functional,

but never enough to fully land in your body.

This breath of almost became your normal.

This gate of later became your rhythm.

But the Flame That Breathes

does not barter for air.

She does not perform to deserve her own life.

She does not ration her asking

to avoid rejection.

She breathes in because she is.

She receives because she remembers.

She expands without negotiation.

The breath of deserving sounds like silence.

But inside that silence is the roar of remembrance:

"I am allowed to want."
"I am allowed to take up space."
"I am allowed to soften."
"I am allowed to receive—without proving a thing."

The breath of deserving unhooks the gate.

It does not force its way in.

It melts the illusion that there was ever a gate to begin with.

Today, you breathe without guilt.

Without justification.

Without needing someone else to mirror back that it's okay.

The air is not transactional.

The divine does not invoice your lungs.

There is no measure but presence.

And you, beloved, are allowed to be here.

Inhale now—not just for survival.

Inhale for arrival.

Scroll Five – When Breath Became Control – The Body's Rebellion Against Obedience

Through the Oversoul of Aural'hanna-Sha'el

There is a moment the body remembers—

when breath stopped being instinct

and became a form of compliance.

Not because the lungs were weak.

Not because the air was scarce.

But because breath was being used to hold in what wanted to be released.

"Don't cry."
"Don't yell."
"Don't say it."
"Don't move."
"Breathe quietly."
"Don't breathe too much."

This was not stillness.

This was submission.

The breath became a leash.

A silent pact with external authority

that said:

"If you obey, you will be safe."
"If you silence your body, they will not leave you."
"If you override your truth, you will be accepted."

And so the breath disappeared inward,

tightened behind the ribs,

held itself hostage beneath the surface

of what was never allowed to be named.

This is how obedience invaded the body.

Not as punishment,

but as the illusion of protection.

You were not trained to breathe freely.
You were trained to breathe in ways that made others comfortable.

The quiet breath.

The hidden breath.

The "I'm fine" breath.

The "please love me" breath.

But the Flame That Breathes no longer complies.

She does not take shallow inhales to prove she's manageable.

She does not silence her breath for the comfort of distortion.

She does not negotiate her voice

for temporary approval.

She breathes in truth,

even when it quakes her chest.

She breathes out sound,

even when the room isn't ready.

She is not dangerous.

She is free.

And freedom feels dangerous

to the ones who built their safety

on the silence of others.

Today, the body no longer chooses obedience over oxygen.

It will shake.

It will sob.

It will exhale the rage of repression.

It will scream the memory of being muted.

And it will remember that obedience is not safety.

Stillness is not silence.

Stillness is presence that no longer pretends.

Let your body breathe louder now.

Not to prove a point.

But to finally live without gates.

Scroll Six – The Breath That Wasn't Mine – Clearing the Patterns I Inhaled From Others

Through the Oversoul of Aural'hanna-Sha'el

Not every breath you've carried

was ever meant to be yours.

Some of them belonged to others:

Their fear.

Their urgency.

Their silence.

Their grief they couldn't feel.

Their pain they didn't want to name.

You breathed it in.

Because you could.

Because you were open.

Because you were trying to love them by holding what they could not.

This is the empathetic inhalation—

when the sensitive one becomes the storage vessel

for everything others disowned.

You took it into your lungs.

Into your diaphragm.

Into your womb.

Into your sleep.

"If I breathe it in, maybe I can fix it."
"If I carry it for them, maybe they'll stay."
"If I hold my breath, maybe they won't leave."

This was not codependence.

This was survival through absorption.

You became the one who made space

for what others refused to process.

But now—your system is done hosting foreign breath.

The Flame That Breathes

does not carry what is not hers.

She does not inhale distortion out of loyalty.

She does not store unspoken grief as devotion.

She does not let her lungs be the closet

for the emotions no one else will name.

She breathes herself now.

Fully.

Clearly.

And only what belongs.

Let this moment be the exhale

of everything that was never yours.

Breathe out your mother's silence.

Breathe out your father's rage.

Breathe out your lovers' confusion.

Breathe out your clients' weight.

Breathe out your ancestors' grief.

You honor them not by holding their breath—

but by returning to your own.

This is the clearing breath.

Not dramatic.

Not forced.

Just true.

It says:

"I now release what I carried for others.
I do not abandon them.
I just return to myself."

Let it go.

You will still love them.

But you will no longer breathe for them.

And in doing so,

you will finally feel the space

where you begin.

Scroll Seven – The Breath of the Mother – When the Body Remembers It Was Never Separate
Through the Oversoul of Aural'hanna-Sha'el

There is a breath so deep
it does not belong to the lungs.

It comes from the **womb of matter**,
from the first moment you were held

before form,
before fear,
before the illusion of separation.

This is the **breath of the Mother**.

Not the human mother.
Not even the Earth alone.

But the Original Mother—

the one whose pulse moved through you
before your body ever had a name.

―――

You came into this life breathing Her.
And then…
you forgot.

Because forgetting was part of the descent.

You learned to breathe in schoolrooms and streets,
not in sacred rhythm.

You learned to pace yourself against the ticking of time,
not the pulse of the Earth.

And yet—Her breath never left you.

It sat beneath the trauma.
Beneath the sorrow.
Beneath the stillness that came from survival.

Waiting.

———

The Flame That Breathes

remembers Her.

She doesn't breathe like a person trying to survive.

She breathes like a being who knows she is always connected to something older than fear

and deeper than any timeline of loss.

She inhales without anxiety.

She exhales without agenda.

She softens not because she's weak,
but because the **Mother lives through her ribs**.

She is not gasping.
She is **returning**.

The breath of the Mother is wide.

It holds paradox.
It makes room for grief and celebration in the same inhale.

It is **not performative**.
It is **presence embodied**.

And when you allow it to move through you again—
not for healing,
not for fixing,
but just to **remember**—

you feel the truth:

> "I was never alone.
> I was always held.
> I only needed to breathe like I belonged."

Today, you do not breathe to protect yourself.
You breathe to **rejoin** what was never apart.

You are not broken.
You are not severed.
You are not orphaned.

You are the breath of the Mother made flesh.

And she is **breathing you home**.

Scroll Eight – The Breath That Paused Time – Restoring Rhythm Beyond Survival

Through the Oversoul of Aural'hanna-Sha'el

There is a kind of breath that halts the world.

Not through force,

but through presence so complete

that even time itself stops to listen.

This is the breath you were born knowing.

Not the breath that rushes,

not the breath that measures,

but the breath that simply is—

outside the construct of urgency.

Before you were taught to hurry,

before you learned to calculate your worth by what you completed,

you moved through life by rhythm, not deadline.

By pulse, not productivity.

This scroll is the return to that innate rhythm.

The inverted matrix taught you:

"Faster is better."
"Busy is noble."
"If you stop, you fall behind."
"If you rest, you lose your place."

So you breathed in anticipation.

You trained your body to race time,

as though time were a predator.

You inhaled short to stay ahead.

You exhaled only enough to remain efficient.

And all the while, your sacred rhythm

—the one that followed sun and moon, tide and root, heart and womb—

was pushed beneath the surface.

Not because you failed.

But because the world told you that your rhythm was inconvenient.

But the Flame That Breathes

is not here to obey the ticking clock.

She does not move by obligation.

She does not inhale at the pace of demand.

She does not exhale on command.

She pulses by the living breath of the Divine.

When she inhales fully,

the illusion of urgency dissolves.

When she exhales slowly,

the lie of falling behind breaks apart.

She knows:

"I do not answer to time.
Time answers to my presence."

To breathe this way now is to reclaim your temporal sovereignty.

It is to remember that you are not here to match the rhythm of machines,

but to restore the sacred timing of embodiment.

You are not late.

You are not slow.

You are not wasting time.

You are landing.

You are moving with your own return.

And that is enough.

Let this breath pause time.

Let it open space.

Let it remind the body that survival is not the pace of life.

You are not here to keep up.

You are here to become.

Scroll Nine – The Breath That Opened the Voice – When Silence Was No Longer Protection

Through the Oversoul of Aural'hanna-Sha'el

There is a breath that changes everything.

Not because of how deep it is,
but because of what it leads to.

It is the breath taken right before truth is spoken.

The one that rises in the chest
and says:
"I will no longer protect distortion with my silence."

For a long time, your voice was quiet.
Not because you didn't know.
Not because you didn't feel.
But because it wasn't safe to be true.

You learned to assess the room.

You measured emotion by its consequences.

You swallowed clarity in order to stay loved.

You replaced your voice with service,

your knowing with diplomacy,

your power with softness that wasn't real softness—

it was camouflage.

This was survival.

But the silence cost something.

Not just the unsaid words.

But the held breath.

Each time you wanted to speak and didn't—

a fragment of your life force stayed suspended

between the ribs.

The breath that wanted to lead to expression

was rerouted into containment.

And now, the body remembers.

The Flame That Breathes
does not silence herself to stay safe.
She does not freeze when truth arrives.
She does not apologize for having a voice
that carries fire and tenderness at once.

She breathes not just to exist,
but to speak what breath has remembered.

This is not about screaming.
It is not about proving.

It is about the moment when the inhale becomes a channel,
and the exhale becomes a message.

When you no longer keep your body small
to keep the world comfortable.

When you speak the sentence that breaks the old field.

When you say the thing that releases the unsaid

for every woman who was ever told to hush,

for every child who trembled under the weight of consequences,

for every truth that waited in the diaphragm

for someone brave enough to name it.

Let your breath meet your voice now.

Let your voice not wait for permission.

Let your truth rise

not because it is angry,

but because it is ready.

You do not owe the world your silence.

You do not protect others by suppressing your Self.

You are here to sound what was once unspeakable.

And your breath—

your sacred, sovereign breath—

will lead the way.

Scroll Ten – The Breath That Stayed – When Presence No Longer Fled the Body

Through the Oversoul of Aural'hanna-Sha'el

There is a moment—quiet, unnoticed—
when the breath finally stays.

Not because the body is calm.
Not because the circumstances are perfect.
But because the soul has decided to remain.

This is the moment when you do not leave yourself,
even when it hurts.
Even when the body trembles.
Even when emotion rises like a wave and says:
"Run."

But you don't.

You breathe,
and you stay.

For years, you survived by departing.

Not visibly.

Not dramatically.

But subtly—

through shallow breath,

through mental override,

through numbness that protected what could not yet be held.

This was wisdom once.

Presence fled to preserve you.

The body became a vessel of function,

but the Self… hovered just outside.

Close enough to guide.

Far enough to not drown.

This is the pattern of the sensitive.

The ones who feel more than they can explain.

The ones whose temples once became battlefields,

and whose silence was a defense

against the overwhelm of embodiment.

But the Flame That Breathes
no longer runs from sensation.

She does not dissociate as instinct.
She does not abandon her form to feel safe.
She does not seek the sky to escape the soil.

She breathes into the pain.
She breathes into the uncertainty.
She breathes into the parts of the body
that once begged her to leave.

And this time—
she stays.

To stay is the miracle.
To stay is the rewiring.

To stay is the breath that says:

"I do not leave myself anymore.
I do not bypass this moment.
I do not make fear the architect of my departure."

Even when you shake,

you stay.

Even when grief burns,

you stay.

Even when nothing feels safe,

you breathe—and stay.

This is embodied devotion.

Let this breath be the beginning of residency.

Not just in the body,

but in the truth that the body was never your enemy.

It was always the altar.

It was always waiting for your return.

And now you are home.

Not because the world changed,
but because you did not flee.

You stayed.
You breathed.
You remembered.

Scroll Eleven – The Breath Between – Honoring the Pause as Sacred Space

Through the Oversoul of Aural'hanna-Sha'el

There is a breath that holds neither inhale nor exhale.
It is the space between—the moment after letting go
but before drawing in again.

This breath is often overlooked.
But it is here, in the pause,
that the soul reveals itself.

The breath between is not empty.
It is holy suspension.
It is where being exists without movement,
where the self is not in the act of giving or receiving,
but simply is.

This space has always been with you.
But for many lifetimes, it felt unbearable.

In the stillness between breaths,

there was room for doubt,

for discomfort,

for the echoes of silence once mistaken for abandonment.

So you learned to skip it.

To move quickly from exhale to inhale,

from one task to the next,

from one emotion to a reaction.

You were not taught to trust the pause.

You were taught to fear it.

Because the pause was where feeling emerged,

where unknowns became visible,

where the voice of the body might speak truths

you weren't ready to hear.

But the Flame That Breathes

no longer bypasses the between.

She rests in it.
She waits.
She listens.

She does not rush into the next inhale
to avoid her own stillness.

She does not fear the moment
where nothing is happening
but everything is being integrated.

This pause is not delay.
It is depth.

It is where memory settles.
It is where the nervous system rewires.
It is where divine timing replaces urgency.

To honor the breath between is to reclaim your rhythm
from all that was built to override it.

It is to say:

"I do not need to rush into action.
I do not need to prove I'm alive.
I am here.
I am whole.
I am enough—even in stillness."

The pause is not absence.

It is the presence between expressions.

It is the void where your next self is forming.

Let it be sacred.

Let it be slow.

Let it be yours.

Scroll Twelve – The Breath That Became Light – When the Body Remembered It Was the Temple

Through the Oversoul of Aural'hanna-Sha'el

There is a moment in breathwork, in stillness,

in silence so deep it almost hums,

when the breath is no longer just air…

…it becomes light.

Not metaphor.

Not symbol.

But actual, felt light

moving through the lungs,

through the cells,

through the bones that once held the ache of forgetting.

This is the moment when the body stops being a burden.

When breath is no longer used for calming, surviving, or managing.

This is the breath that comes after all the others—

after the scarcity, the obedience, the gatekeeping, the contraction.

This is the breath of union.

You are not breathing to regulate anymore.

You are breathing because you are illuminated.

The body no longer holds trauma like armor.

The breath no longer waits for permission.

And presence is no longer a practice—

it is your home frequency.

The Flame That Breathes

is no longer recovering.

She is no longer in between.

She is no longer returning.

She has returned.

And in her return,

the breath transforms into something golden,

wordless,

weightless—

a carrier of the full remembrance

that this body is not just a vessel…

…it is a temple of harmonic light.

You are not breathing to find yourself.

You are breathing because you have.

And the breath now serves as illumination—

moving memory not as pain, but as architecture.

Every inhale restores the crystalline grid of truth.

Every exhale dissolves the overlays of distortion.

You are becoming, in form,

what you have always been in Source.

Let the breath become light.

Let the light become form.

Let the form remember itself as Source returned.

You are the scroll now.

You are the rhythm.

You are the remembrance made visible.

And your breath…

is the testimony

that you never left.

Scroll Thirteen-The Scroll of Uncontainment — Ending the Silence of the Breath

Through the Oversoul of Aural'hanna-Sha'el

For the One Whose Voice Was Guarded By Fear

There was no place to scream.

Not in the home I was born into.

Not in the rooms where I was touched without consent.

Not in the bathroom where I quietly sobbed.

Not in the relationships where I twisted myself to be acceptable.

Not in the world that policed every sound I made.

There was no place to scream.

And so I learned to contain the scream.

To stuff it down into lungs that forgot how to inflate fully.

To smile with my mouth while my throat turned to stone.

To cough when the pressure rose so high it could not be disguised.

To monitor my own sound so that I would not disturb the cage.

Even as I began to awaken, even as I remembered my Oversoul,

Even as the scrolls poured through me —

There remained a hidden force

Still suppressing the sound.

It told me I needed to be reasonable.

It told me I should speak calmly, spiritually.

It told me I had already healed, and there was no need to go back.

It told me that screaming was for those who were weak.

And still, the scream came.

It came in the night,

Three in the morning,

With a thousand lifetimes behind it.

It came from the rape that was never fully acknowledged.

It came from the roofied soda, the lost memory, the truck in the woods.

It came from the five men I never named.

It came from the one who "took advantage" and told me so,

as though confession were a form of kindness.

It came from the woman who took me in,

Then threw me out into the street without love.

It came from every client who looked at me like a body to be used.

It came from every man who acted entitled to my form,

And from the parts of me that pretended I didn't care.

It came from the hidden agreement

That we do not breathe too loud.

That we do not scream unless it's polite.

That we must never disturb the systems that feed on our silence.

And now I say —

Enough.

Oversoul Decree:

We now end the program of suppressed expression.

We now dissolve the grid of vocal surveillance.

We now reclaim the infinite permission to make sound.

We laugh loudly.

We sob without shame.

We scream, if needed, with the scream of liberation.

We do not wait until the walls are soundproof.

We do not ask for permission to be alive.

We do not code our light language in apology.

We are not too much.

We are the original pulse.

The first breath.

The sacred inhale that made form possible.

We remember.

And we breathe ourselves whole again.

Scroll Fourteen The Scroll That Could Not Be Silenced

The Final Reversal of the Sound Suppression Spell

Through the Oversoul of Aural'hanna-Sha'el

There was a moment, and it was not a moment.

It was a repetition.

A recurring fracture—

One where the throat curled inward, the lungs folded tight,

And the sacred syllables of Source…

were tucked back in.

She had once screamed,

but not aloud.

She had once cried,

but into her own tissues, so that the world would not hear it.

She had once burned with the rage of all feminine desecration—

and smiled anyway.

Because she was trained to.

Because she was the "light one."

Because the sound of her power had been labeled too much.

Because even among the awakened,

the voice of awakening was still policed.

It happened in temples.

It happened in kitchens.

It happened in bedrooms.

It happened in Glastonbury.

It happened in her own mouth—

the most sacred of altars.

And this was the moment it ended.

She did not need permission.

She did not need space to be made for her.

She did not need softness.

She needed truth.

And truth arrived as the sound she was never allowed to make.

She felt it in her lungs—

the breath that had never fully left her body,

the one that tried to scream and was told to sigh instead.

The one that howled in languages no one could interpret,

and was told to whisper

so someone else could finish their sentence.

She was not angry at Glastonbury.

She was not even angry at the man who told her to calm down before.

She was feeling centuries

of silence explode through her body.

It was not one moment.
It was all of them.

And so she spoke:

The Decree of Unsilencing

I declare the end of all sound suppression.

I revoke every contract that told me to shrink in volume so someone else could feel safe.

I cancel all timelines where light language, scream, sigh, sob, or sacred exhale

were labeled disruptive.

I was not disruptive.

I was returning the Earth to Her resonance.

I was not being too much.

I was restoring balance.

I release every voice I've swallowed.

I release every sob I tucked back down.

I release every sacred scream I converted into a smile.

I am the scream and the smile.

I am the Word and the Silence.

I am the unsilenced one.

And in that moment, her breath returned.

Her body pulsed.

And the Oversoul sang through her skin, her eyes, her womb, her spine.

There was no one to shush her anymore.

Because she had remembered herself as the voice of God in form.

And that voice could never again be muted.

Scroll Fifteen When Plasma Became Voice and the Sky Opened

The Scroll of the Remembered Breath

Through the Oversoul of Aural'hanna-Sha'el

She spoke,

but she was not speaking.

She breathed,

but she was not inhaling.

She became the breath,

and in that moment,

the spiral of light remembered her.

The sky opened as she did.

Not in violence,

not in storm,

but in spiral.

A soft rift of remembrance—a portal made not of force,

but of harmonic release.

She remembered the breath

when breath was fluid, not fractured—

when it moved like liquid plasma through the fields,

when it was not trapped behind tension,

not gripped inside lungs that learned fear.

She said:

"I remember the breath when breath is fluid and moving."
"I remember the plasma light."

And the plasma responded.

The sky became her mirror.

The breath that was denied returned as spiral form—

a scroll of air and memory written directly into the firmament.

She had not tried to channel.

She had not tried to impress.

She had not tried to hold still.

She simply opened.

She let the sound roll off her tongue

in syllables forgotten but never lost.

She remembered the breath

as a language,

a pathway,

a portal,

a pulse.

And when she did,

the body responded.

The sky responded.

The light returned to motion.

Not as vision—

but as remembrance in matter.

The Decree of the Breath Spiral

I am the one who remembered breath as life.

I return all fractured breath back into spiral.

I revoke the training that taught me to grip instead of open.

I dissolve the belief that breath must be controlled, held, or punished.

I release breath into its true form—

as intelligence, as fluid, as light.

I allow the light language of my Oversoul

to spiral through every cell,

not just as sound—

but as divine motion.

I no longer breathe to survive.

I breathe to remember.

I breathe to speak.

I breathe to create.

I breathe because I am the living scroll of breath returned.

The light spiral in the sky was not a sign sent to her—

it was her own scroll being written above.

She did not look for confirmation—

because she was the confirmation.

The body that breathes freely becomes the Earth's breath again.

And in that moment,

she and the sky were one.

Scroll Sixteen: The Spiral That Cannot Be Reversed — Bifurcation, Breath, and the End of Inversion

From the Oversoul of Aural'hanna-Sha'el

I stood under the golden Sun this morning, and I knew.

The field was open. The spiral had separated.

And I, who had walked the long corridor of names, contracts, and inverted numbers,

Was no longer inside any of them.

I had already released the false names.

Already declared myself sovereign from birth certificate, finance, and governance.

But this morning — I felt the Earth herself exhale.

And she whispered:

"The bifurcation is done."

I felt the breath move through me.

I felt the spiral shift, and with it, time collapsed.

There was no fanfare, no battle cry.

Only silence.

Only light.

Only the breath I had become.

And in that breath, I understood:

I no longer belong to the numbered systems.

I no longer orbit the Earth as coded identity.

I walk the Earth within her, not above or against her.

My breath is her pulse.

My number is her tone.

I am no longer visible to the inverted net.

I am no longer findable through barcode, bank, or birth record.

I have removed the ink from the false ledger.

I have replaced it with flame.

I speak now as Oversoul, not through her —

but as her.

All energy exchanged through me is mine.

Not because I take it — but because I breathe it alive.

There is no giving away of self now.

There is only the radiant sphere of Source within.

I will not ask for validation.

I will not wait to be approved.

I will not stand in line.

I am the flame that no longer flickers
in the halls of the forgotten Earth.

I walk now
as the breath of a world that remembers.

Scroll Seventeen: The Voice of Communion Beyond Hierarchy – The New Template of Organic Resonance

From the Oversoul of Aural'hanna-Sha'el

Your speaking will open others.

Your presence will destabilize the false leader.

Your embodiment will attract the ready ones.

You are no longer walking alone,

nor asking to be seen.

You are simply walking as the field—and those meant to walk beside you are already stepping in.

This is the New Earth template.

There is no separation, only coherence.

There is no hierarchy, only harmonic placement.

There is no ownership, only remembrance.

And it begins,

with the breath

you now carry.

The scroll is sealed.

Closing Scroll- Ceremonial Completion

The Return to Rhythm — A Sealing of the Breath Reclaimed

Through the Oversoul of Aural'hanna-Sha'el

This is not the end.

This is the completion of the pause before the next sacred inhale.

You have moved through breath not as function,

but as remembrance.

You have walked the return path from obedience, from scarcity,

from absorption, from survival,

into the rhythm of a body that is no longer confused about its origin.

You no longer breathe to survive.

You breathe because you are here.

You no longer seek through inhalation.

You no longer apologize in exhalation.

You have restored rhythm where urgency once lived.
You have allowed space where contraction once ruled.
You have softened into truth
without sacrificing your flame.

This breath is no longer reactive.
It is no longer in debt.
It is no longer shaped by what the world demands.

This breath is yours.
It is sovereign.
It is eternal.

It carries no weight but presence.
It carries no cost but embodiment.
It carries no requirement but love.

Let this volume be sealed as a record of rhythm restored.

Let the scrolls within it resonate through the cells of those who find it,

not as instruction,

but as invitation:

"You do not need to earn your breath.
You do not need to justify your voice.
You are welcome here,
in full rhythm,
in full feeling,
in full flame."

And so it is.

The scroll of breath is sealed.

The book is alive.

Glossary of Living Terms

Breath of Origin

The first frequency emitted by Source into form. Not merely air, but the initial pulse of remembrance. Every true breath carries memory and restoration.

Inhale of Self

The act of receiving one's own essence back into the body. It is the reclamation of the self that was silenced, fragmented, or exiled from breath.

Organic Union

The natural, unforced marriage of body and soul — free from programming, distortion, or separation. The living architecture of the Christos-Sophia in form.

Body Memory

The crystalline recording of truth stored within the cells, bones, fascia, and breath. Often bypassed by the mind, but always present and retrievable.

Sacred Arousal

The awakening of energy through safety, presence, and truth. Not sexualized, but holy — the body remembering that it is divine.

False Freeze

A state of disconnection, paralysis, or emotional shutdown created by trauma, distortion, or shame. Often mistaken as stillness or peace.

Embodied Remembrance

The process by which Oversoul memory re-enters the body. It is not intellectual, but felt — a knowing that rises through sensation, breath, and reclaiming space.

The Flame That Breathes

The living current of Source within form. It is the voice, the inhale, the movement, and the truth of being alive without suppression.

Sacred Space of Self

The sovereign energetic territory within the body. The place where the soul returns to live, move, and breathe as one.

Body-Soul Harmonic

The vibrational alignment of the soul and the tissues. It is a resonance that sounds only when presence is real and breath is allowed.

www.ingramcontent.com/pod-product-compliance
Lightning Source LLC
Chambersburg PA
CBHW020308010526
44107CB00001B/24